Book 2

A Logical Approach to Spelling

Highly Structured Curriculum based on the sound
in words and the application of spelling rules.

Jurina Dean

Thank you

And so, the journey continues...

A big thank you again to my three older children. Your help with designing the logos has been invaluable. You're all such talented artists! Jemimah, thank you for your continuous enthusiasm and love for working in your Mamma's books. And of course, a big thank you to my husband for standing by me every step of the way. I love you all so much!

Index

Preface

Welcome to the journey of helping your child learn to read and write in English! I invite you to pause and take a moment to explore this preface, as it sets the stage for the incredible impact this book can have on your child's learning experience.

As a mother of four living in Geneva, Switzerland, I understand the unique challenges and opportunities that come with raising children in a multi language environment. My eldest daughter breezed through her weekly spelling lists, effortlessly mastering each word. However, my second daughter faced a different path. The frustration she experienced with her spelling lists was palpable. While she could learn words, recalling them a week later felt like an insurmountable task.

After discovering that she had dyslexia and short-term verbal memory challenges, I embarked on a five-year journey of learning and discovering how to work through the curriculum using an alternative method.

I was advised to focus on the 300 most frequently used words in English. We dedicated a year to mastering these words, achieving a 50% success rate. While this was a start, I knew there had to be a better way. My daughter excelled in math, successfully following logical steps to solve problems. This inspired me to research a logical approach to spelling.

In my quest to find effective resources, I explored many different books and countless online materials. I realised that a vast amount of these resources lacked the structure and repetition necessary for lasting retention.

While I couldn't find a single definitive resource, I began piecing together a beautiful method for learning to spell in English—one that emphasises a logical structure, much like maths. This book aims to provide that framework.

In English spelling, we often encounter exceptions to the rule, but we'll tackle these later in our journey. Initially, we focus on what makes sense phonetically and explore homophones as a key theme throughout this book. Together, we'll play detective, investigating the fascinating world of different spellings. As a child's brain develops, they will naturally anchor these "exception to the rule" words.

Our curriculum provides a strong foundation and support for visual memory and logical thinking. We cover all spelling elements of national curriculums, but with a difference — we emphasise the sounds in words and foster confidence in blending simple words for future success.

We'll explore "borrowed" words from other languages, highlighting the similarities that can serve as helpful anchors. Towards the end of the series, we'll address words that often cause confusion early on for children who find spelling challenging. These words will align correctly in your child's mind as they mature, so we won't focus on teaching them prematurely. Instead, we'll nurture their spelling confidence in stages of mind-readiness.

At the end of each section, you'll find a word bank. Use this to create spelling tests until your child masters each word, revisiting it throughout the series. Be mindful of your child's attention span, and keep lessons between 10 to 30 minutes a day. Consistent, short repetitions are key! Help them understand why words are spelled a certain way, and revisit the word bank after a month, and again after three months.

You are making a wonderful difference to your child's learning journey! Enjoy every moment of this experience—it truly passes quickly. Happy learning together!

Reading and Spelling - Book Two

Every child is unique and learns at a different pace. It's perfectly fine to revisit exercises from Book One to ensure a solid grasp of the material before moving on. . We explored phonetic blending and sentence construction in detail. Book 1 serves as a solid foundation that will support our learning in this book

In Book Two, we'll cover diphthong sounds, where two vowel letters make the vowel say its name. Short spelling tests will help reinforce this learning. We'll also look at specific letters at the end of words and delve into the use of c, k, and ck, along with soft sounds for c and g. Additionally, we'll explore the relationship between q and u, and study the doubles: ff, ll, ss, and zz.

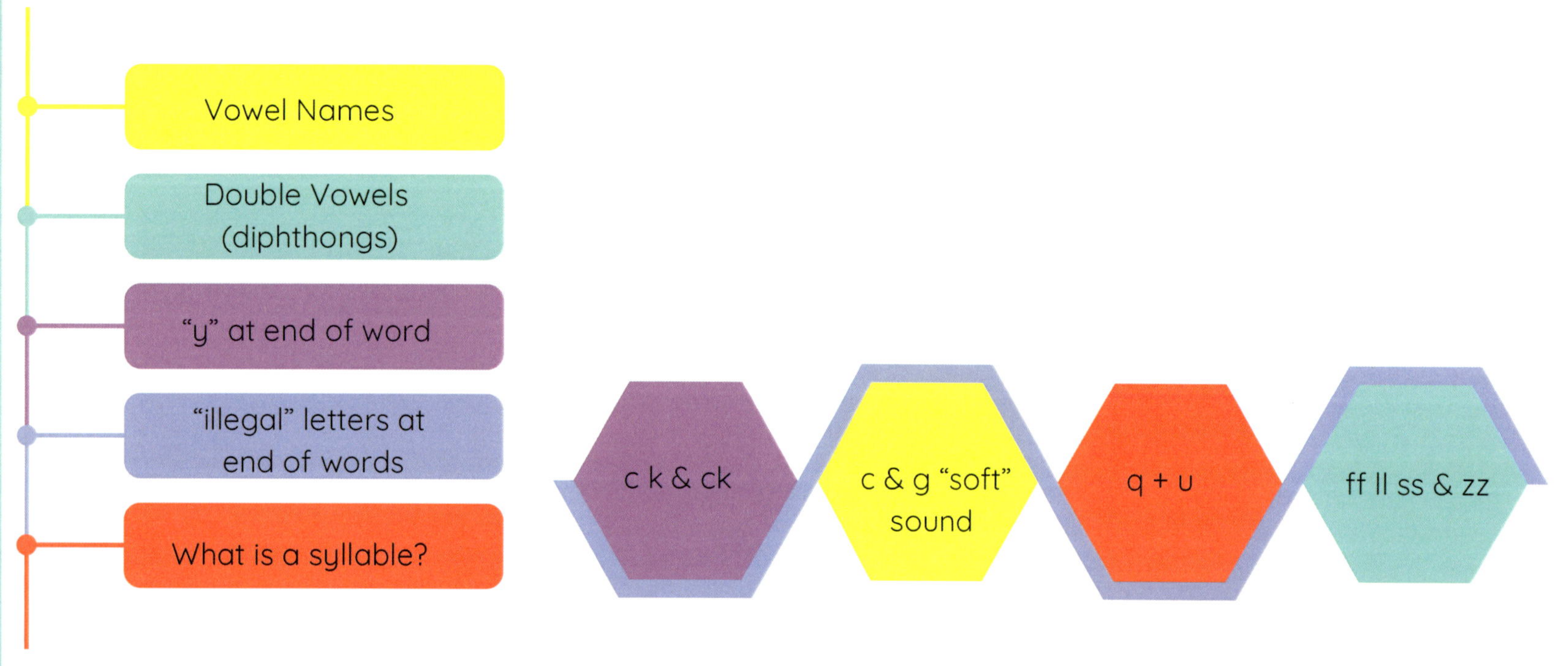

Tips

It's important to take things step by step! First, let's focus on mastering the sounds of the alphabet before introducing their names. This will help build a strong foundation for blending sounds as we read and write. Once your child is confident with the sounds, we can gently introduce the five vowel names (like a for acorn). Remember, knowing the ABC song isn't necessary for learning to read or write first words; understanding the sounds each letter makes is key. We will look at the vowel names in this book.

As we progress, let's ensure your child is comfortable with small letters before moving on to capital letters. Capital letters are special and are mainly used for names and at the beginning of sentences.

When it comes to print and cursive letters, let's take our time! Mastering print letters first will help avoid confusion, especially with letters like b and d.

Happy spelling!
Jurina Dean

What a typical week with this book looks like

Daily practice in reading, writing, and spelling is essential, and it should be fun! Pay attention to your child's focus and adjust as needed. Think of their attention span as a muscle that we're gradually strengthening. We can create a consistent structure for lessons or mix things up based on your child's energy and mood. On some days, starting with a spelling test followed by new activities can work well. Reading should ideally be a separate session, especially if it's longer than five minutes. Let's keep lessons short—no more than 30 minutes without reading.

Make sure to celebrate each achievement, no matter how small! Remember, the key is to review concepts regularly and keep the learning experience joyful.

To summarise

1. Learning a concept once a week, reviewing it daily
2. Spelling test 5-20 words (to succeed, you have to set short spelling tests at least twice a week.)
3. Exercises
4. Reading 5-30 mins a day

Levels of mastering reading and spelling

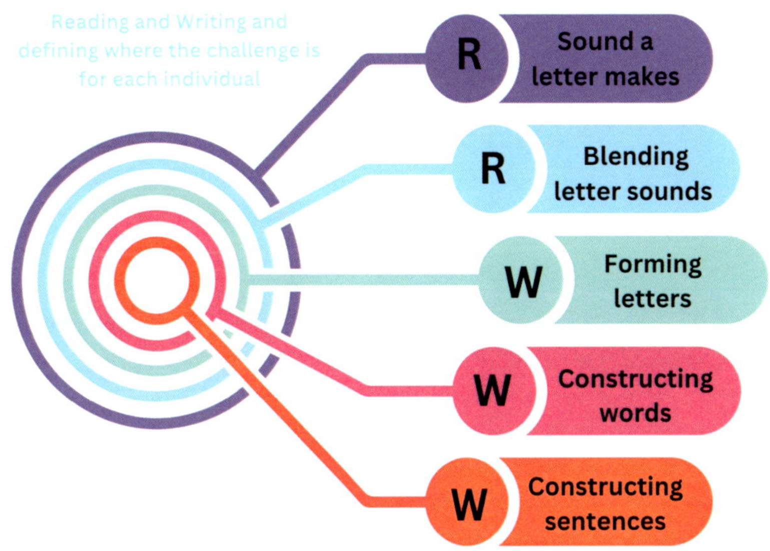

If your child ever finds an exercise to be a bit challenging, don't worry! You can make it easier by simplifying one of the skills involved. For instance, writing a sentence utilises all the skills mentioned above, but by using words that are already written down, your child can focus on one skill at a time while still learning, creating, and building their confidence.

This approach can also be applied to word-building. With already formed letters, your child can create words more easily. By "stripping out" some of the complexities of a task, you can help identify specific areas that may need extra attention.

It's important to remember that every child is unique in the way they learn. Some may find blending words to be a bit tricky, while they might excel at forming letters, and vice versa. Likewise, some children may be able to construct a sentence beautifully in conversation but may need more support when it comes to writing it down.

By teaching from multiple strength points, we can truly enhance the development of each individual child. Together, we can create a supportive learning environment that encourages growth and confidence!

apple
fan
jam
nose
rabbit
van
boot
goat
whale
cat
kick
orange
snake
horse
leaf
pen
tail
x-ray
doorknob and the door
yo-yo
eggs
igloo
mum
quick
umbrella
zoo
It is important not to say the name of the letter, but the sound it makes! Not "A" for acorn but "a" for apple.
a b c d e f g h i j k l m n o p q r s t u v w x y z

Vowels
a e o u i

Letter **sounds** are different from letter **names**.
Every vowel letter can be associated with at least 2 sounds!

SHORT SOUND   SOUND

a e i o u

in

apple, egg, insect, orange, umbrella

LONG SOUND   NAME

where the letter says its name A E I O U
We will refer to the name of a letter by putting it in brackets

{A} {E} {I} {O} {U}

{A} in acorn, {E} in equip, {I} in ipad, {O} in program, {U} in united

Circle all 5 vowels in each row. Cover the previous line when doing a new line. Practise 1-2 lines a day.

a b c d e f g h i j k l m n o p q r s t u v w x y z

a b c d e f g h i j k l m n o p q r s t u v w x y z

a b c d e f g h i j k l m n o p q r s t u v w x y z

a b c d e f g h i j k l m n o p q r s t u v w x y z

a b c d e f g h i j k l m n o p q r s t u v w x y z

a b c d e f g h i j k l m n o p q r s t u v w x y z

a b c d e f g h i j k l m n o p q r s t u v w x y z

a b c d e f g h i j k l m n o p q r s t u v w x y z

a b c d e f g h i j k l m n o p q r s t u v w x y z

a b c d e f g h i j k l m n o p q r s t u v w x y z

The "a" for apple -   says its name "A"

The "e" for egg - says its name "E"

The "i" for igloo - says its name "I"

The "o" for orange - says its name "O"

The "u" for umbrella - says its name "U"

acorn

emoji

item

oh!

universe

Practice this!!!
Refer to the ABC
song here...

The "y" is our cameleon. It changes colour.
Sometimes it is a vowel like the a e i o u and
other times it prefers to be a consonant.

Often the "y" helps out the "i".

Our other helper is the "e" ,
"e" comes to the rescue, when we are in a
sticky situation.

Double vowel sounds

Practise the **names** of the letter sounds.

{A} ai ay 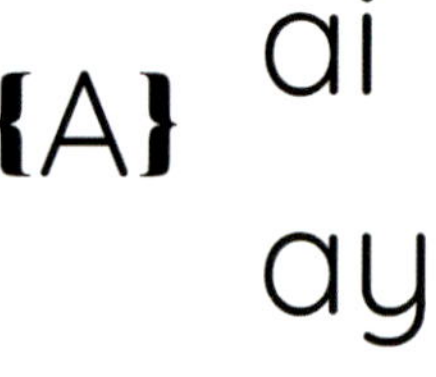 **a**corn

{O} oa oe  **o**cean

{E} ee ea  **e**moji

{U} ui ue  **u**niverse

{I} ie  **i**pad

Double vowel sounds

Let`s get familiar with double vowel sounds being in the middle of the word.
What can you hear in the beginning and at the end of the word?
Write the missing letters to each word.

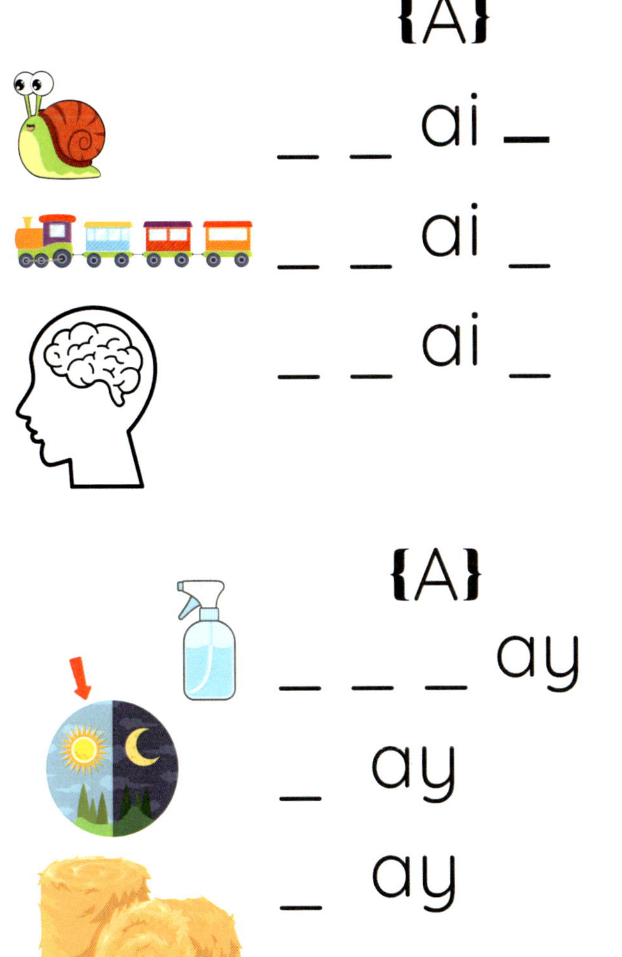

{A}

_ _ ai _

_ _ ai _

_ _ ai _

{A}

_ _ _ ay

_ ay

_ ay

{E}

_ ee _

_ _ _ ee _

_ _ ee _

{E}

ea _

_ ea _ _

_ ea

Double vowel sounds

Let`s get familiar with double vowel sounds being in the middle of the word.
What can you hear in the beginning and at the end of the word?
Write the missing letters to each word.

{O}

_ oa _

_ oa _

_ oa _

{I}

_ ie

_ ie

_ _ ie s

{O}

_ oe

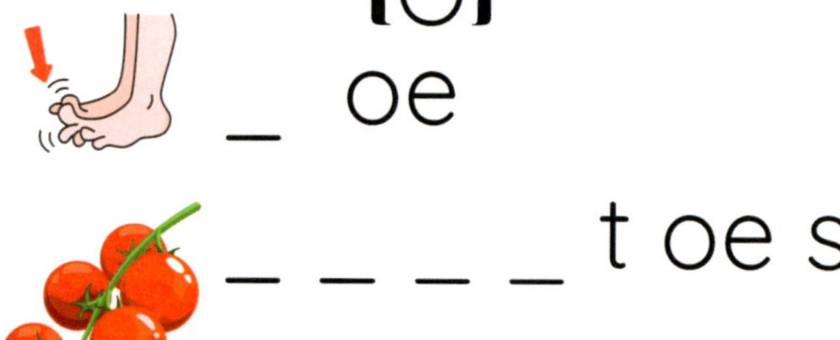

_ _ _ _ _ t oe s

_ _ ie _

Double vowel sounds

Let`s get familiar with double vowel sounds being in the middle of the word.
What can you hear in the beginning and at the end of the word?
Write the missing letters to each word.

Mixed

{U}

_ ui _

_ ui _

_ _ ue

_ _ ue

_ _ ` _ _ _ue

_ _ ai _

_ _ _ ay

_ _ ee _

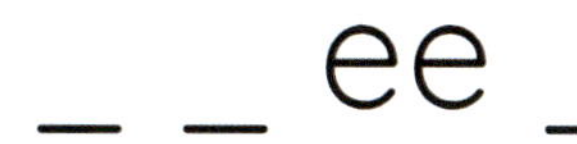

_ ea

_ _ oa _

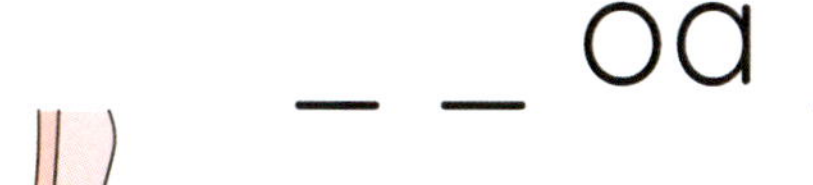
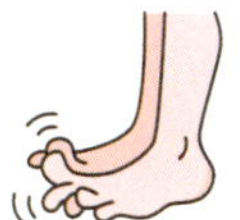

_ oe

_ ie

_ _ ui _

_ _ ue

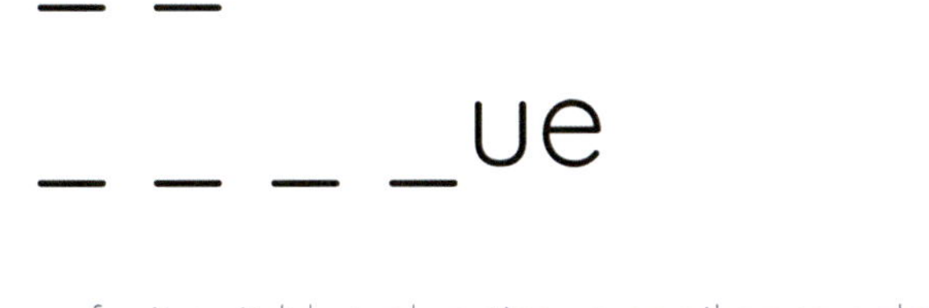

fruit suit blue clue tissue snail spray sleep tea float toe pie fruit glue

Double vowel sounds

Connect each picture to the correct double vowel sound. The vowel saying its name.

Double vowel sounds

Connect each picture to the correct double vowel sound. The vowel saying its name.

oa
oe {O}

ie {I}

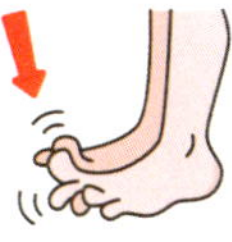

Double vowel sounds

Connect each picture to the correct double vowel sound. The vowel saying its name.

ui
ue **{U}**

ai
ay **{A}**

Double vowel sounds

Connect each picture to the correct double vowel sound. The vowel saying its name.

ai
ay
{A}

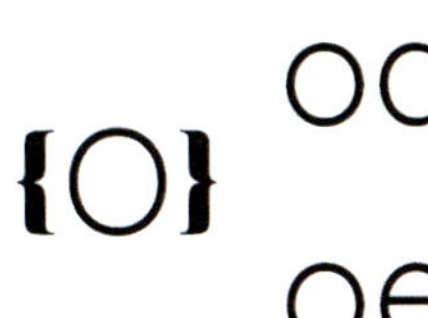

{O}
oa
oe

{I} ie

ee
{E}
ea

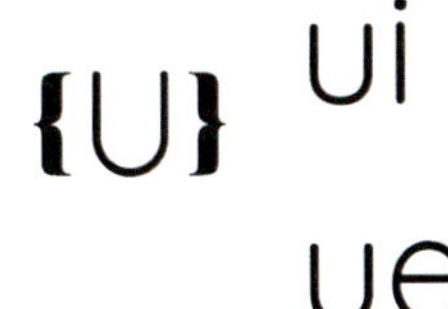

{U} ui
ue

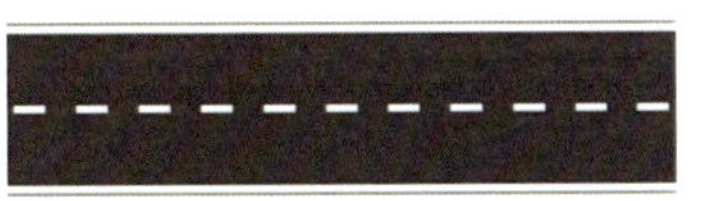

Double vowel sounds

Cover the pictures on the right. Read the words on the left and check if you are correct.

{A}

sn ai l

tr ai n

br ai n

{E}

f ee t

str ee t

sl ee p

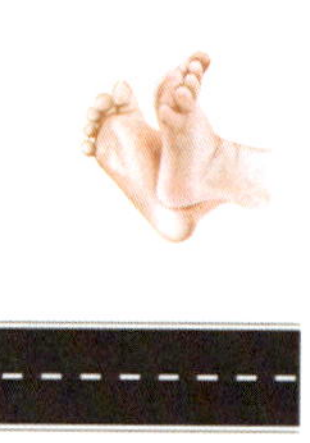

{A}

spr ay

d ay

h ay

{E}

ea t

p ea ch

t ea

Double vowel sounds

Cover the pictures on the right. Read the words on the left and check if you are correct.

{O}

b oa t 

g oa t 

fl oa t 

{O}

t oe 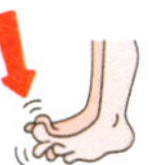

to ma t oe s 

{I}

p ie 

t ie 

fl ie s 

fr ie s 

{U}

fr ui t 

cl ue 

tis s ue 

Word search

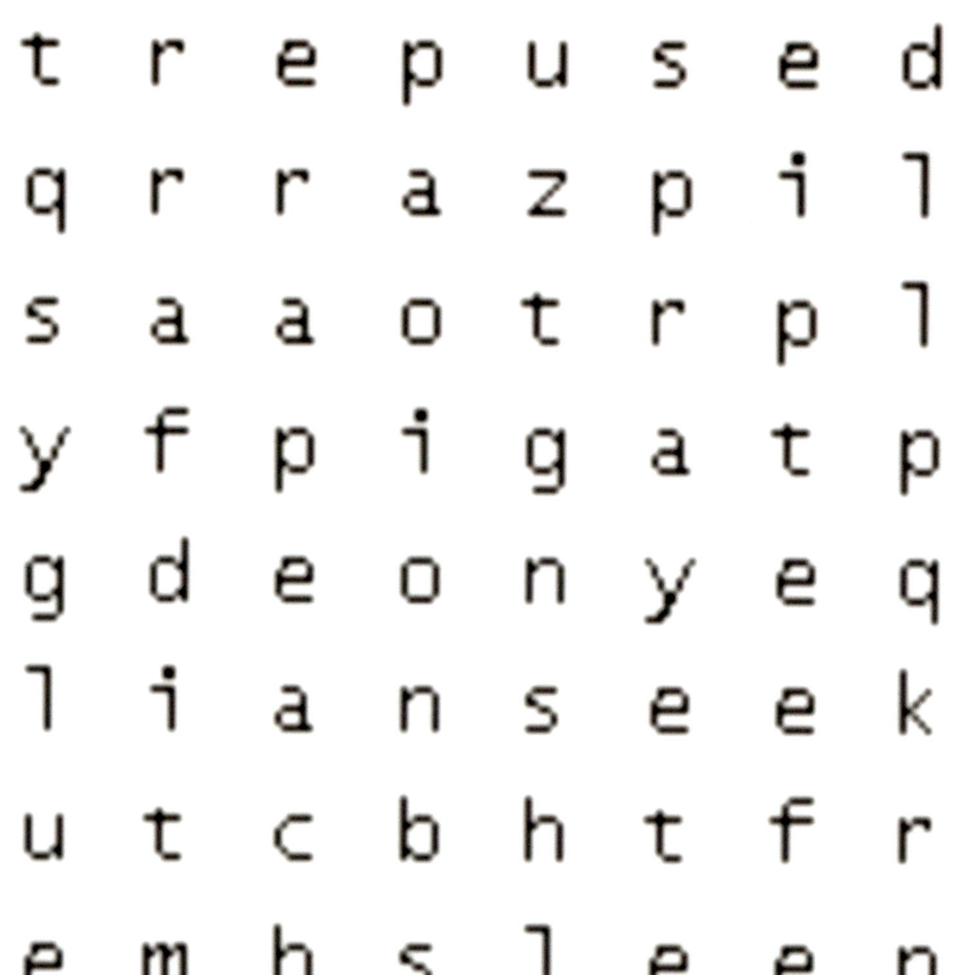

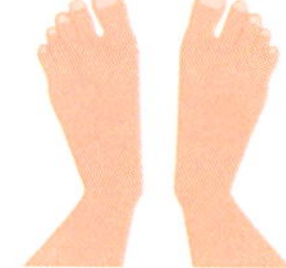 

eat
float
goat
pray
snail
feet
fruit
peach
sheep
spray
flies
glue
pie
sleep
train

Word search

cheese
cherry
watch
chess
thick
thin
this
that

e	a	k	l	j	c	s	t
q	q	v	v	h	k	s	h
y	r	r	e	h	c	e	a
l	t	e	h	k	c	h	t
g	s	h	c	c	t	c	u
e	q	i	i	i	t	z	f
t	h	i	n	s	r	a	q
t	c	j	d	a	c	q	w

Word search

d	v	d	k	r	b	s	d
z	f	b	i	e	o	q	e
b	a	l	l	r	i	o	b
h	b	l	w	b	t	b	d
k	s	e	d	a	e	a	h
m	x	b	b	v	u	t	r
v	a	t	h	z	l	h	i
g	o	d	h	y	b	z	x

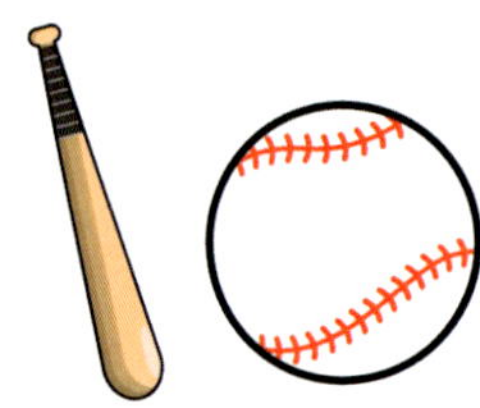

desk
door
blue
bat
ball
dirt
bath
bell
dog
dam
bed

Reading

tray	sleep	eat	fries	toe	glue
hay	green	easy	pie	foe	true
clay	keep	each	tie	potatoes	blue
stay	street	read	die	tomatoes	fruit
spray	feet	Easter			suit
day	teeth	clean			
play	wheel	peach	my	goat	
say	bee	east	try	boat	quit
crayon	tree	neat	fly	coat	quick
betray	sweet	deal		road	quack
away	*three	tea		oak	
today	*free	least		soap	
holiday	fee	yeast		loaf	ill
hooray	meat	cream		toad	kill
train	meet	dream			fluff
daisy	been	team			cuff
plain	bean	jeans			kiss
chain		please			miss
wait		cease			buzz
paint		crease			
maid		grease			
rain		leash			
rein		weasel			
reign		feast			
tail					

"illegal" letters at the end of a word

Depending on the age of the child, you can come back to this concept later.

illegal letters

five letters that are not permitted
to be at the end of a word in
English

i j q p u v

"**e**" & "**y**"
to come to the **rescue**!

i	pi	pi**e**
j	oranj	orang**e**
q	plaq	plaqu**e**
u	tru	tru**e**
v	giv	giv**e**
v	lov	lov**e**
i	tri	tr**y**
i	plai	pla**y**

We will refer back to these "illegal" letters often.
This rule will become more clear as we progress.

The "y" is our cameleon. It changes colour.
Sometimes it is a vowel like the a u i e o and
other times it prefers to be a consonant.

Often the "y" helps out the "i".

Our other good helper is the "e"
"e" comes to the rescue, when we are in a
sticky situation.

Illegal letters

5 letters that are not permitted to be at the end of a word in English......

i j q p u v

We rely on the letter "**e**" & "**y**" to come to the **rescue**!

- i (pi   pi**e**)
- j (oranj   orang**e**)
- q (plaq   plaqu**e**)
- u (tru   tru**e**)
- v (giv   giv**e** lov   lov**e**)

---

illegal letters
...that is why....

tri	try	hav	have
fri	fry	abov	above
unti	untie	weav	weave
		lov	love
tru	true		
glu	glue	uniq	unique
		arrang	arrange

soft "g" = j

Ooooooopppppppsssss!

There will always be exceptions ....but we are learning the general pattern first

Exceptions: menu flu fungi ski hi ... a lot of these are what we like to call "borrowed" words from other languages, cultures, fashions, science or abbreviations

---

Vowels

Every word must have a vowel
&
Every syllable must have a vowel

a   e   i   o   u

& "chameleon" y

"y" is the chameleon in the alphabet. Often it acts as a vowel and sometimes as a consonant.

- Letter **sounds** are different from letter **names**
- Every vowel letter can be associated with at least 2 sounds!
- SHORT SOUND   SOUND
  a e o u i
- LONG SOUND   NAME
(says its name A E O U I)
We refer to the name of the letter by putting it in brackets
{A} {E} {O} {U} {I}

Challenges with phonetic awareness can be overcome by reading word blending specific letters. Especially no-sense words, to reinforce "read the sound you see"
eg ble scre scro tro tre fle fli etc

"illegal" letters at the end of a word

Fill in the missing letter.

lov _

lov _

lov _

lov _

lov _

lov _

lov _

lov _

lov _

lov _

lov _

Our other good helper is the "e"
"e" comes to the rescue, when we are in a
sticky situation.

Long vowel sounds "diphthongs" summary

<table>
<tr><td>

When two vowels go walking, the first one does the talking ➡ ...it says its name

a + i   ai {A}
a + y   ay {A}

- train
- brain
- pay
- clay

</td><td>

When two vowels go walking, the first one does the talking ➡ ...it says its name

o + e   oe {O}
o + a   oa {O}

- toe
- foe
- goat
- float

foe or friend

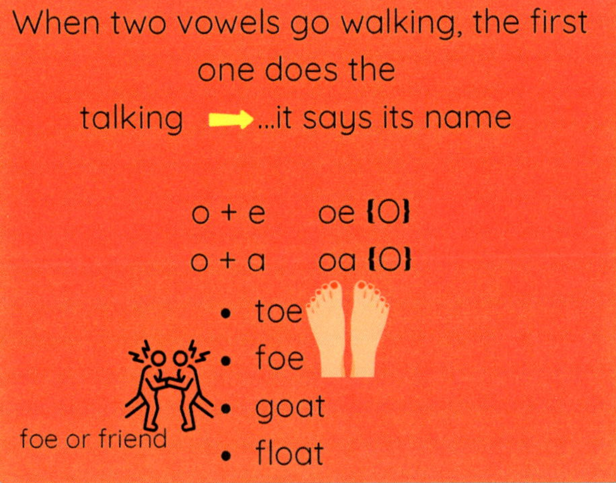

</td><td>

For a short vowel sound to say its name, you can add an "e" on the end of a word.

a _ e   {A} • brak   brake
e _ e   {E} • delet   delete
o _ e   {O} • brok ➡ broke
i _ e   {I} • strik   strike
u _ e   {U} • flut   flute

</td></tr>
<tr><td>

When two vowels go walking, the first one does the talking ➡ ...it says its name

e + a   ea {E}
e + e   ee {E}
e + y   ey {E}
e + i   ei {E}

- team
- green
- honey
- sheikh

</td><td>

When two vowels go walking, the first one does the talking ➡ ...it says its name

i + e   ie {I}

- tie
- pie
- die

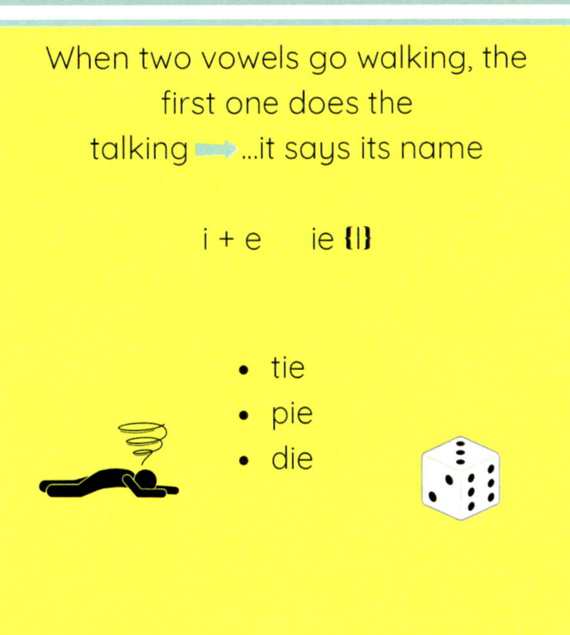

</td><td>

When two vowels go walking, the first one does the talking ➡ ...it says its name

u + e   ue {U}
u + i   ui {U}

- glue
- true
- fruit

</td></tr>
</table>

Two Vowels

When two vowels go walking, the first one does the talking
➡ ...it says its name

a + i   ai {A}
a + y   ay {A}

{A}

{A}

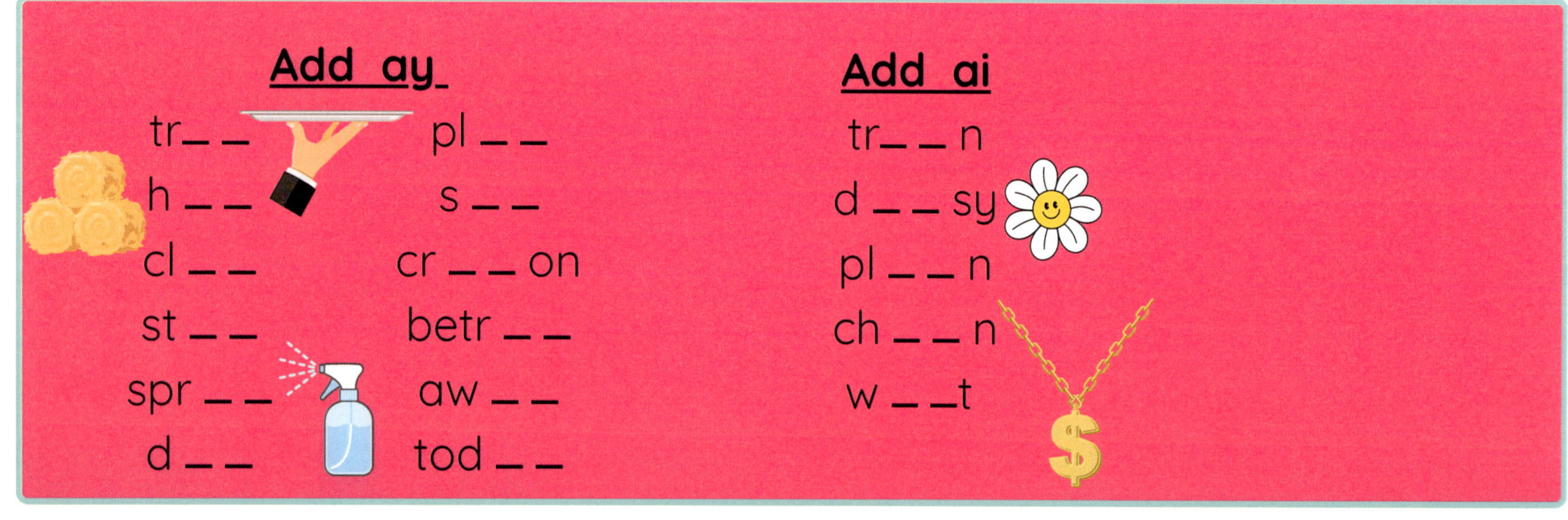

Practise some words

7 different ways to spell the sound {E}

We are still looking at all the vowels that are walking together, but it is important to point out that the **name** of "e", {E} (in the word **e**mail) can be spelled 7 different ways.

1. e + a ➡ ea {E} — team dream sea
2. e + e ➡ ee {E} — sleep see feet
3. e_e ➡ {E} — swede delete
4. e + y ➡ ey {E} — hockey money
5. y at the end of the word {E} — happy lucky
6. e + i ➡ ei {E} — receive ceiling
7. e / mail (open syllable word) — email

We will look at all of them. "ei" spelling will be studied later.

Two Vowels

When two vowels go walking, the first one does the talking ➡ ...it says its name

e + a   ea {E}
e + e   ee {E}
e + y   ey {E}

Add ea

_ _ t
d _ _ l
_ _ ch
t _ _
cl _ _ n
p _ _ ch

Add ee

b _ _
sl _ _ p
f _ _ t
k _ _ p
str _ _ t
sw _ _ t

Add ey

k _ _
kidn _ _
monk _ _
donk _ _
hon _ _
mon _ _

Sydn _ _
Disn _ _
chimn _ _
hock _ _
jock _ _

ey {E} is rare. Most of the time, we only write "y" when we hear the sound {E} at the end of a word. More on that later.

Two Vowels

You need to build "anchors" - ways to remember whether the word is spelled with "ee" or "ea".

sl_ _p

We stay lying down when we sleep all night.

gr _ _ n ee

k _ _ p — Keep the same...

str _ _ t — All street markings looks the same.

f _ _ t — Both feet the same.

t _ _ th — Teeth are all the same colour.

Add ee

wh _ _ l — Both wheels are the same.

*b _ _ _

**kn _ _ — Both your knees look the same.

tr _ _

sw _ _ t — Sugar grains are all the same

thr _ _   3

fr_ _

f _ _

*Be and bee: Ask your child to write both and emphasise the sound the bee makes...bzzzzzzzzz...... with a long "e" = {E}

** knee and know we will look at later, but teach saying the "k" sound every time you ask to spell knee. Eg. Write knee...remember: "k"nee for knee

Add ea

Eat different things.

_ _ t

_ _ sy — Some things are not easy, they are different

_ _ ch — Remember Easter is with a capital letter. We get different celebrations, therefore "ea".

_ _ ster

cl _ _ n

p _ _ ch — One ripe peach One rotten peach

_ _ st

n _ _ t

d _ _ l — more than 1 side to a deal

t _ _ — cup and saucer different

l _ _ st

b _ _ st — One friendly, the other not so friendly.

We put "anchors" down when learning to write the {E} sound to help remember when words are written with "ea" or "ee".

sp _ _ k — Speak to different people every day.

fr _ _ k

tw _ _ k

y _ _ st — Suncream and cream with fruit is different.

cr _ _ m

dr _ _ m — Dream different dreams every night.

j _ _ ns — Black jeans and blue jeans are different colours.

pl _ _ se — Please in many different languages.

c _ _ se

cr _ _ se

gr _ _ se — Engine grease and food grease is different.

l _ _ sh — Long leashes and short leashes are different.

Spelling test

Two Vowels

When two vowels go walking, the first one does the talking

➡ ...it says its name

o + e   oe {O}
o + a   oa {O}

There are more {O} sounds but we will get to them later

Add oe

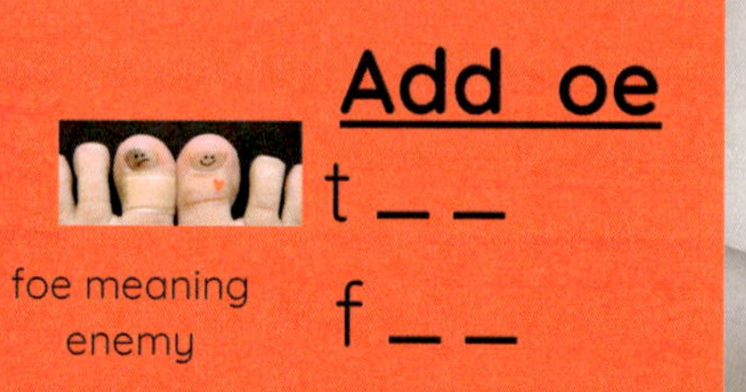

foe meaning enemy

t _ _

f _ _

potat _ _ s

tomat _ _ s

her _ _ s

Add oa

g _ _ t
b _ _ t
c _ _ t
r _ _ d

_ _ k
s _ _ p
l _ _ f
t _ _ d

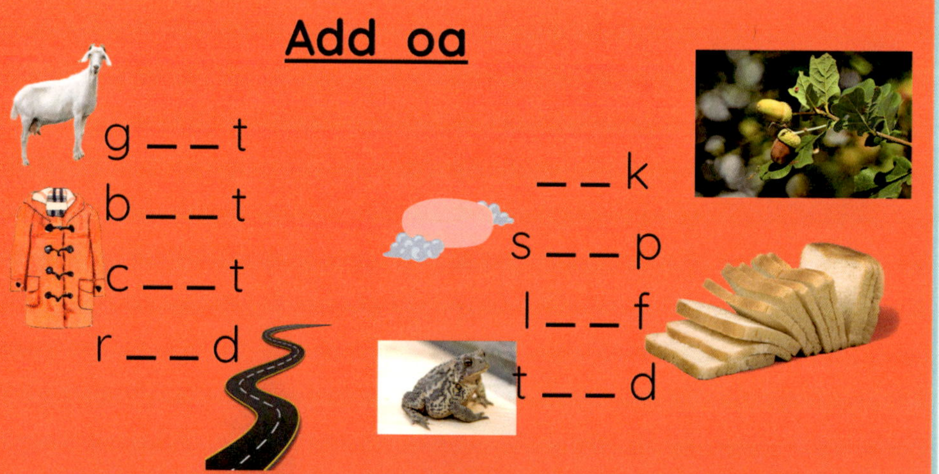

Spelling Test

Two Vowels

Two Vowels

When two vowels go walking, the first one does the talking ➡ ...it says its name

i + e   ie {|}

Add ie

p _ _
t _ _
d _ _
fr _ _ s

"i" can not be at the end of a word so "y" comes to the rescue! It replaces the "i".

mi   y = my
tri   y = try
cri   y = cry
fri   y = fry

Two Vowels

There are more words with the spelling "ui" but they do not make the same sound. These fall into the "non-logical" words category.. We learn them later words when the brain is more developed. (e.g. build, guilty, guide)

Long vowel sounds

For a short vowel sound to say its name, you can add an
"e" on the end of a word

a _ e   {A}
e _ e   {E}
o _ e   {O}
i _ e   {I}
u _ e   {U}

- brak
- delet
- brok
- strik
- flut

- brake
- delete
- broke
- **strike**
- flute

Silent "e"

A silent "e" on the end makes the vowel sound says its name

{A} {E} {I} {O} {U}

{A}

sn _ k _
t _ l _
s _ l _
dr _ n _
sh _ k _
mist _ k _
fr _ m _
infl _ t _
g _ m _
s _ m _
p _ n _
t _ m _

{E}

del _ t _
th _ s _
sw _ d _
concr _ t _
th _ m _

- Very important that these sounds get practised together. The word **envelope** is more challenging but we pronounce it phonetical for the first two syllables and remind yourself an envelope has 3 elements to it (front, back and flip)….3 "e" letters in the word.

{I}

l _ t _
s _ t _
k_t _
d_v_
h_v_
ch_v_s

l_f_

{O}

n _ s _
b _ n _
r _ p _
h _ m _
ph _ n _
n _ t _
gl _ b _
t _ n _
envel _ p _
r_ d _
h _ p _
c _ n _ 

{U}

fl _ t _
r _ d _
c _ t _

HINT! Repeat the same phrase for a cetain word every time.

Long vowel sound

An "e" on the end of a word makes the vowel sound say its name.

Add the vowels a e i o u and the special "e" at the end of each word.

sn _ k _
t _ l _
s _ l _
dr _ n _
sh _ k _
mist _ k _
fr _ m _
ph _ n _
r _ p _
fl _ t _

b _ n _
s _ l _
n _ s _
g _ m _
s _ m _
p _ n _
h _ p _
c _ n _
t _ m _

del _ t _
th _ s _
sw _ d _
concr _ t _
th _ m _

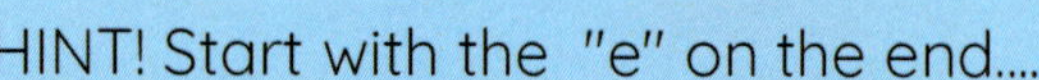

HINT! Start with the "e" on the end....

Word search

```
y a d o t p w x e g
c n o y a r c x m y
e a w c l a w t a e
c k m s e y a r r t
s l a e n i t e f a
e y a t l a m i t k
v r w y s a k y a s
s a m e g i a e m w
e n a l p w m y e e
i d e k a h s h a y
```

came
frame
mistake
same
snake
tame
wait
clay
game
plane
shake
tail
today

away
crayon
hay
pray
skate
tale
tray

Word search

```
b  e  q  h  g  t  b  h  d  n
e  e  m  c  c  l  e  a  n  f
a  r  e  a  n  h  e  a  r  u
s  h  s  e  s  r  f  e  s  r
t  t  a  a  x  y  a  e  y  e
k  a  e  w  t  k  s  o  e  a
q  l  l  o  e  s  m  a  k  l
w  t  p  v  w  e  a  s  e  l
t  s  a  e  f  f  r  e  e  y
t  e  e  r  t  s  g  t  y  y
```

each
fee
keys
read
tea
tweak
beast
easy
freak
leash
really
three
weasel

clean
feast
free
please
street
tree
yeast

Word search

```
k p g e e k q d s b
z x h n n u c s o e
o w o o e o e a a p
r r t s n o c a p o
d o t v t e o x j h
b p a a h e r o e s
j e m d n t i u q q
i o r o q u i c k t
t s s n k z e n o b
b e e n v e l o p e
```

bone
nose
rope
cope
envelope
quick
quit
heroes
phone
soap

drone
hope
quest
road
tomatoes

Spelling test

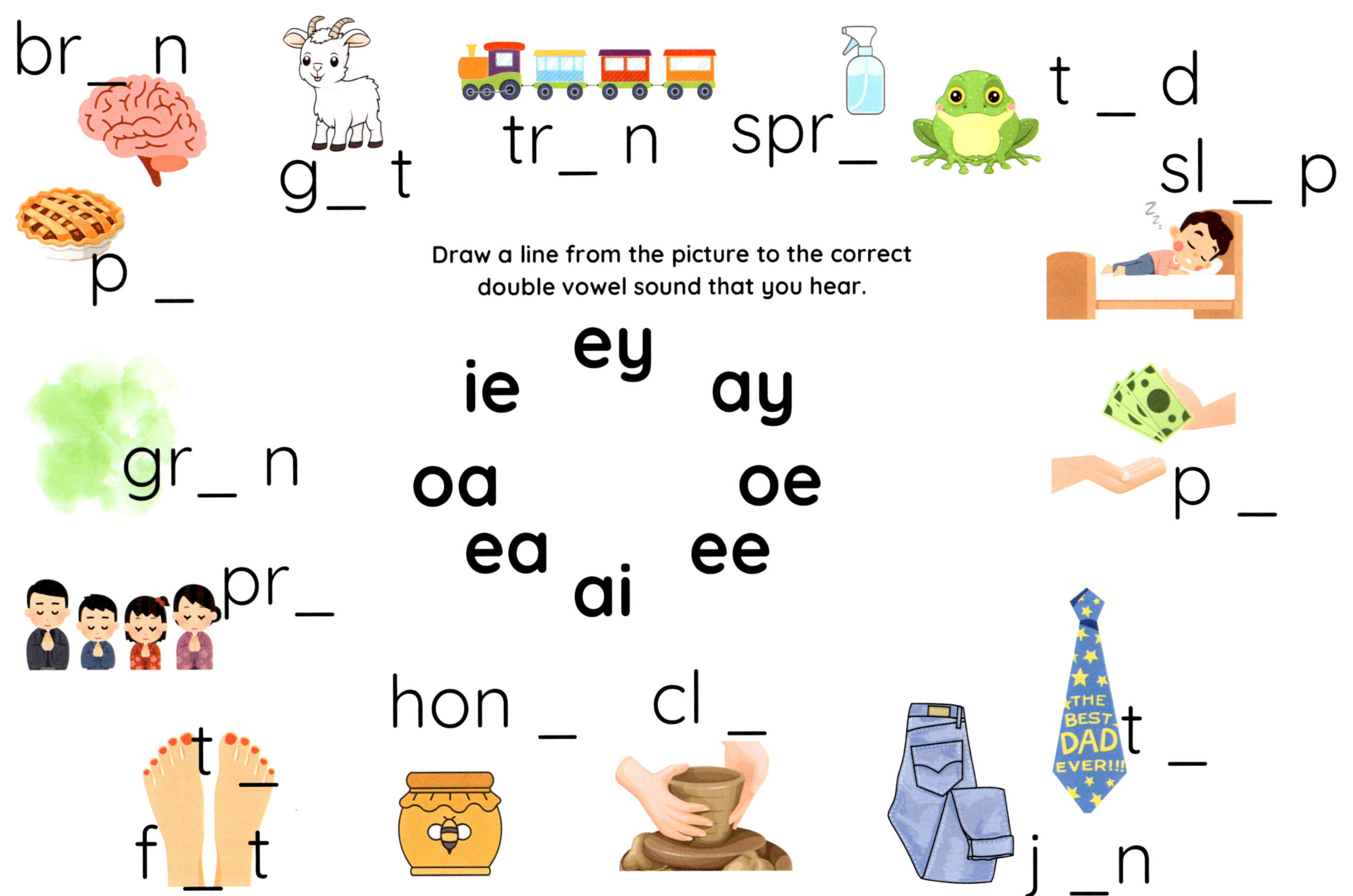
br _ n
g _ t
tr _ n
spr _
t _ d
sl _ p
p _
Draw a line from the picture to the correct double vowel sound that you hear.
ey
ie
ay
gr _ n
oa
oe
ea
ee
ai
p _
pr _
hon _
cl _
t _
t _
f _ t
j _ n
THE BEST DAD EVER!!!

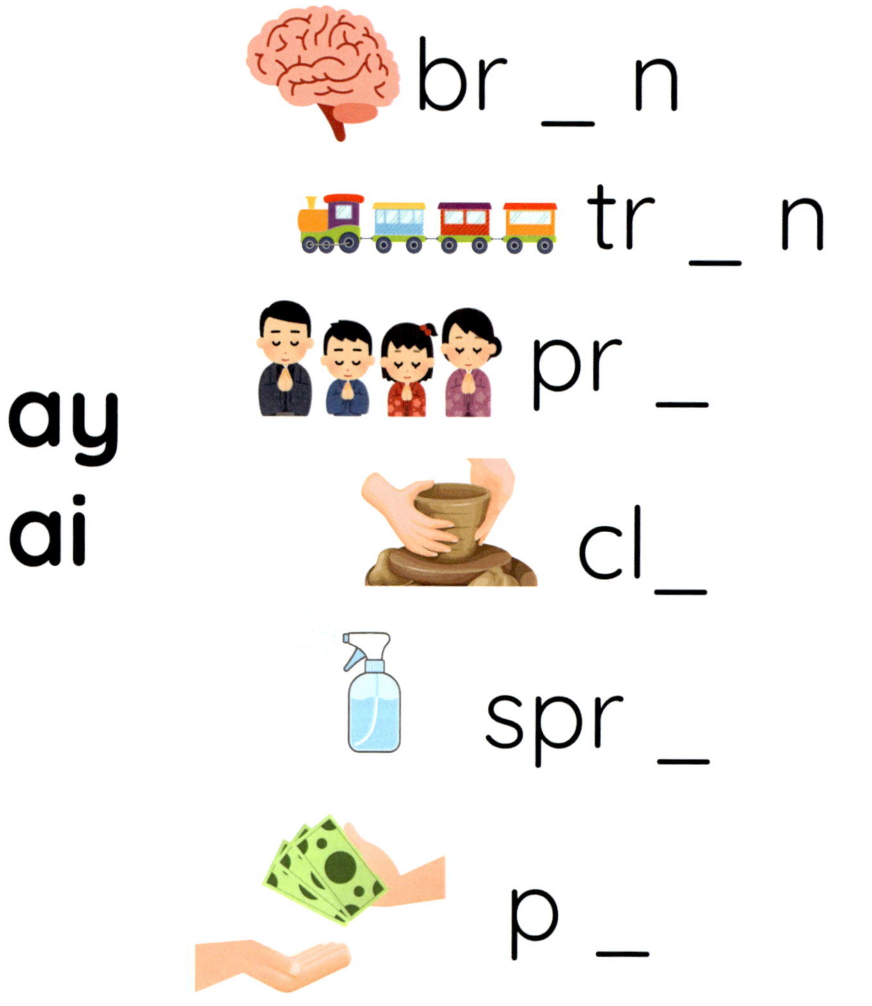

br _ n
tr _ n
pr _
cl_
spr _
p _
ay
ai
Compelte each word to match the picture.

t _ d
g _ t
t_
f _ t
gr _ n
hon_
j _ n
sl _ p
oa
oe
ey
ee
ea

cr _ _ on 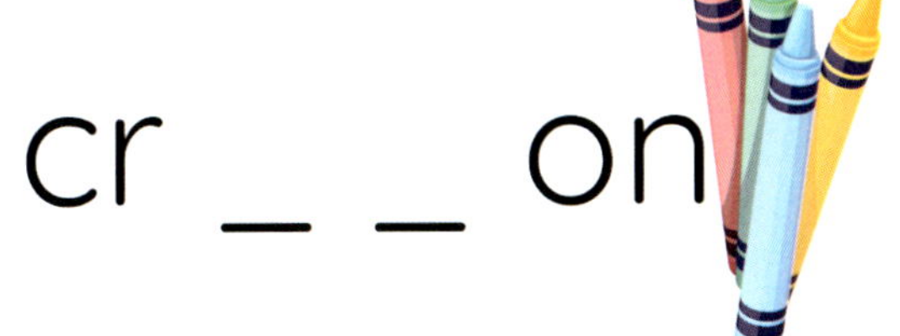

m _ _ l

oo

b _ _ t

ay

h _ _

a_e

r _ p _

ai

m _ n _

s _ _ l

ay

oa

s_ _ p

oa

o_e

m _ _ n

ai

t _ _ 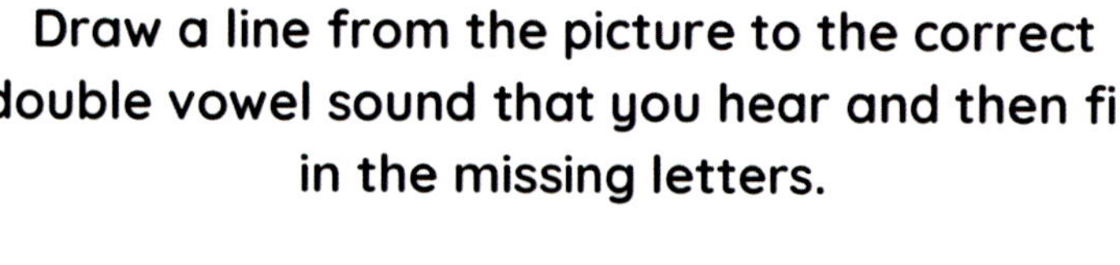

fr _ _ t 

d el _ t _

gl _ _

i_e
ea
i_e
ue
ui
ee
ue
e_e

bl _ _

wh _ _ l

d _ v _

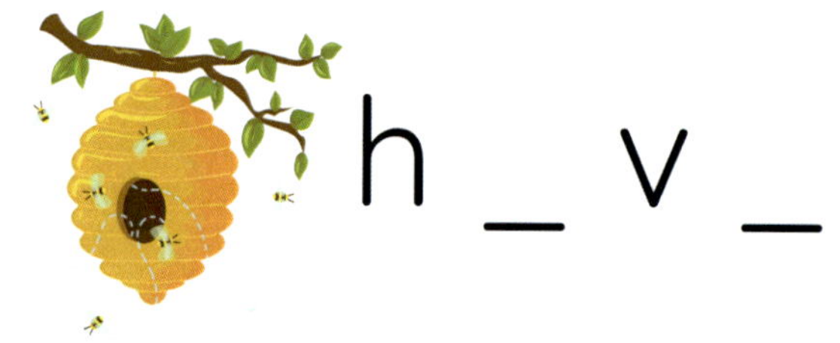
h _ v _

Let us have a bit of fun.....

What is the longest word in the Oxford English Dictionary?

pneumonoultramicroscopicsilicovolcanoconiosis

pneu mo no ul tra mi cro sco pic si li co vol ca no co ni o sis

A 45-letter word for a lung disease, more commonly known as silicosis.

Success in spelling comes with daily repetition of spelling rules and writing the words. A little bit everyday, goes a long way.

to

too 

two **2** 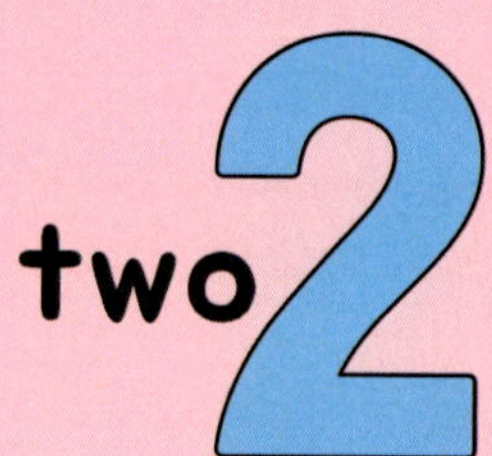

 one **1**

won

be

bee

Can I come to the park too, when I am two?
If you can do one sum in maths, you can have some sweets.
Only one person won the race.
For us to win, the four of us have to work together.
The bee wants to be happy.

sum +

some

2 + 2 = 4

for
four 

1.Cut these out. 2. Match the words to the pictures.3. Match the picture to the double vowel sound that is correct.

ee	jeans	oo	moon	oi	oil
	tree		spoon		soil
	teeth		broom		boil
	feet	ai	train	oy	boy
ea	dream		sail		toy
	sea		tail		oyster
	peach	ay	tray	a_e	plane
	read		spray	e_e	swede
oa	goat		clay	i_e	slide
	toad	ie	pie	u_e	flute
	boat		tie	o_e	globe

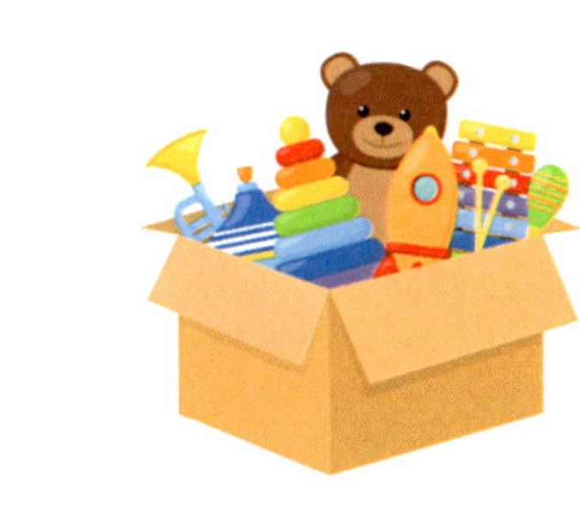

Let`s look at the letter "y"

The "y" is a bit like a plaster for any wound ….. it makes everything better!

When you hear the sound {E} at the **end** of a **2 syllable word,** then often, the word has a "y" at the end.

happy

sadly

lucky

boldly

many

teeny

tiny

pretty

really

study

family

many

lady

story

only

very

easy

The "y" also helps out the "i" at the end of a word as we discussed previously.

boy (instead of boi)

toy (instead of toi)

deploy (instead of deploi)

Sometimes words are spelled with an "ey" at the end to make the {E} sound but these are exceptions.

The "y" gets fired from its job at times. You will see that when we look at plural forms.

berry becomes berri+es = berries

The "y" is not needed anymore as the "i" is no longer at the end of a word.

But this is for later.

Write a few sentences using the words above. We will practice them together with all the other {E} sounds.

Let us talk about that ....y

Rewrite these sentences below to practice the {E} sound
spelled with a "y" at the end of 2 syllable word.

I am happy. It is a teeny tiny bug. The lady is very lucky. She wrote a really good story. The family has many dogs. She is a very pretty girl.

Vowels

Two vowels saying

oi !

o + i → oi
o + y → oy

- <u>"i" cannot be at the end of the word</u>, Therefore, "oy" is used for words ending in "oi".

<u>Add oy or oi to the words to make the sound "oi!"</u>

b _ _   b _ _ l   h _ _ st

t _ _   t _ _ l 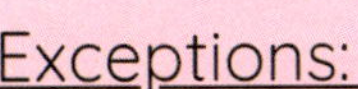   p _ _ n t

j _ _   s _ _ l   m _ _ st

ann _ _   c _ _ n   sp _ _ l

enj _ _   j _ _ n   v _ _ ce

j _ _ nt   ch _ _ ce

Exceptions:

r _ _ al

l _ _ al

_ _ ster

 v _ _ age

Rolls R _ _ ce

- Study these exceptions. They are such a class of their own, that it is easier to anchor the spelling of these words here and ask your child to name 5 words that don't follow the "oi" rule.

- A completely standalone word we teach here is buoy. Remind your child every time when writing this word, that it is a float in the water to rescue or warn you.

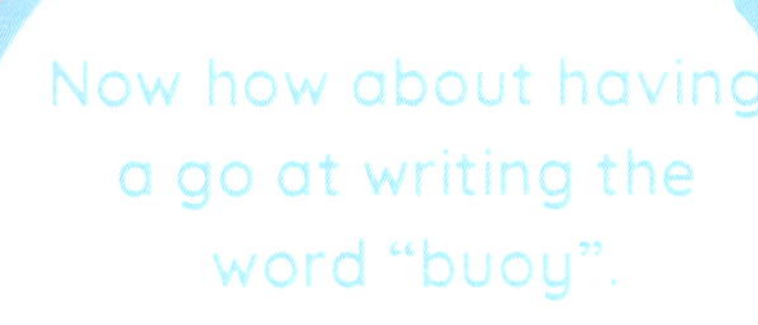

Write down all the ways you can spell the following sounds
Don`t forget a_e:

{A}

1. _______
2. _______
3. _______

{E}

1. _______
2. _______
3. _______
4. _______
5. _______
6. _______

{O}

1. _______
2. _______
3. _______

{I}

1. _______
2. _______

{U}

1. _______
2. _______
3. _______

oi

1. _______
2. _______

Word search

```
y o t v m a r s y c
t q d n o l e a o h
r m i j o i n t n o
y o e p p f c l n i
c z u n l f b e a c
u s r y c o r t i e
r e t s y o e u z s
o i s d y u d u i o
r r p a l o d i l t
a f l b p a j a e g
```

boy
joy
die
fruit
royal
true
annoy
choice
fly
glue
oyster
tie
try

blue
coin
fries
joint
pie
toy
voice

Crossword

Across

2. It is a precious metal. (steal,steel)

6. You can go to jail if you _.

7. monkee or monky or monkey

8. He was only _ years old when he learned to swim. (three,free)

10. There are 7 days in a _. (weak,week)

11. I took the _ of the horse to control it. (rains,reigns, reins)

12. The beach is very hot in summer. (see,sea)

14. I fell on the ground and hurt my _. (nee,knee,nea)

Down

1. The _ stung me and hurts (be,bee)

2. The price was marked down. It was on _. (sail,sale)

3. He loves playing a _ with his dad. (gaim,game)

4. She _ the truth. (speeks,speaks)

5. The king _ in his kingdom. (rains,reins,reigns)

9. Can you _ more specific in your answer. (be,bee)

11. There was a lot of _ and wind yesterday. (rane,rain)

13. He is too _ to walk up the hill. (weak,week)

Crossword {E} sound

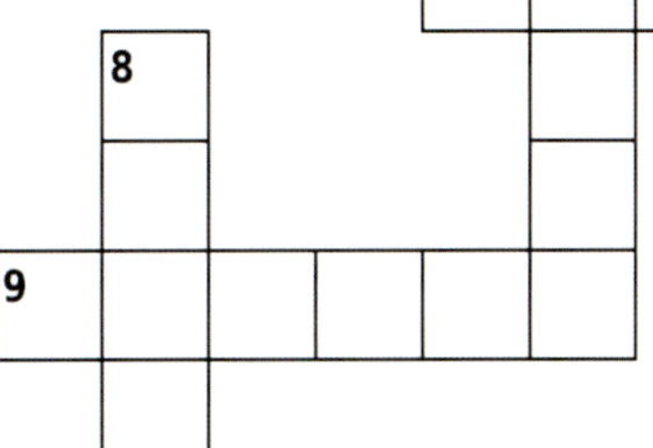

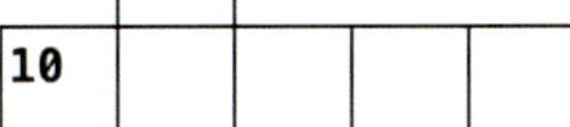

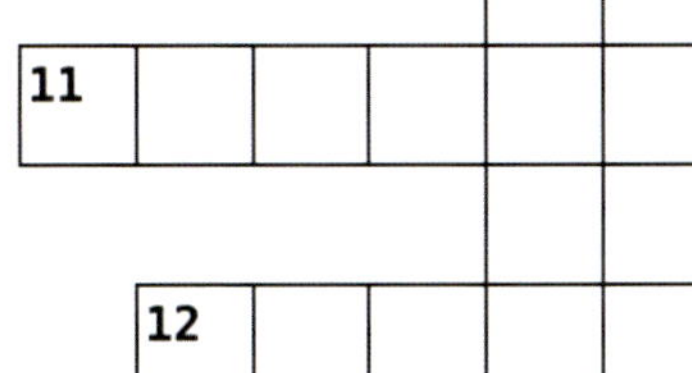

Across

2. You have to brush them often. 

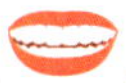

5. Trousers that *are* most often blue. 

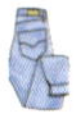

7. You need this to buy things.

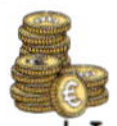

9. My brother, sister, mum, dad and I are called f... 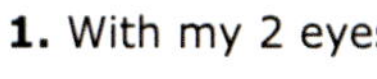

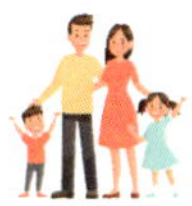

10. White and sometimes black.

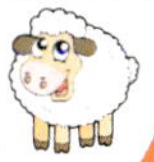

11. Sport we play on grass or ice.

12. The number. 

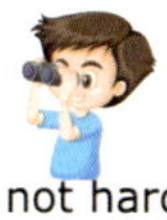

Down

1. With my 2 eyes.

3. When things are not hard they are _ _ s _

4. Are you sad or happ_?

6. The bee makes this. 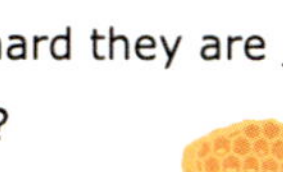

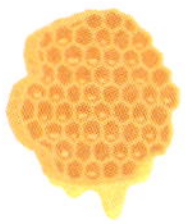

8. A fruit. 

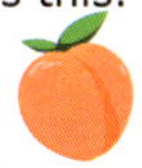

10. A vegetable.

Circle the correct spelling

One day there was a goat/gote that liked potatos/potatoes and tomatos/tomatoes. He didn`t like sweed/swede or grainy beens/beans. His favourite food was oisters/oysters. He was a real pane/pain when he was hungry. His tail/tale was brown, his teath/teeth were white and his knows/nose was black.

If he could take a voyage/voyige and sale/sail around the gloab/globe, he would go from Sydney/Sydnee to disney/Disney/Disny. He didn`t have even one coyn/coin or a toi/toy to play with. He was a happy goat. Always full of joi/joy and loved playing the floot/flute.

His best friends were a monkey/monkee/monky and a tode/toad. They all loved going to the see/sea. One night, they were dreeming/dreaming about being a teem/team with a fortuun/fortune and attitude/atitude. Instead, the tree/three/free of them drank tee/tea maid/made with cleen/clean water.

Spelling dictation double vowels

He reads a book. She likes tea. We fly on a plane for a holiday to Sydney. He plays hockey at home.

Rewrite these sentences in preparation to a spelling test.

Spelling dictation double vowels

She writes a note and puts it in an envelope. Will you join us for a party? He bakes a cake. The boy broke my crayon. The monkey eats all the tomatoes and swedes.

Rewrite these sentences in preparation to a spelling test.

Spelling dictation double vowels

The bees make honey and we pay money for it. She gave him a quick kiss. He eats a peach, oysters and fries. We read our books and then clean our teeth. We went to Disneyland for Easter.

Rewrite these sentences in preparation to a spelling test.

A vowel says its name

When a vowel is at the end of a first syllable, we call it an open syllable.
When a consonant is at the end of a syllable, we call it a closed syllable.

acorn
equal
email
even
d**e**lete
pr**o**gram
m**u**sic
ipad

acorn = a + corn
Two syllables, first syllable ends in a vowel "a" =
called an **open syllable**

The vowel in an **open syllable** says **its name**

{A} in acorn

popcorn = pop + corn
Two syllables, first syllable ends in a
consonant "p" = called a **closed syllable**

apple = ap + ple
Two syllables, first syllable ends in a
consonant "p" = called a **closed syllable**

So "a" in apple sounds "a" and not
its name {A}

Vowel at the end of a first = open syllable syllable.

then

the vowel says its name!

acorn	a/corn
uniform	u/ni/form
item	i/tem
equal	e/qual
ebook	e/book
even	e/ven
delete	de/lete
program	pro/gram
music	mu/sic
ipad	i/pad

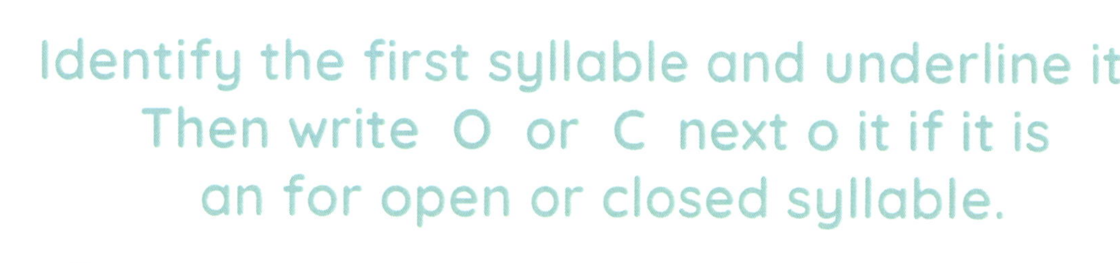

<u>a</u>corn O
maple
<u>rab</u>bit C
paper
coffee
kitchen
camping
imax
equal
idea
minor
bookshelf
program

picnic
center
silly
computer
ebook
blanket
drummer
photo
music
pencil
remote
lampshade
eggshell

uniform
pebble
table
carpet
even
potplant
pretty
iPad
baby
item
delete
maple
raven

Word search

```
e  d  e  l  e  t  e  c  n  a
q  g  t  f  v  s  o  r  r  t
u  l  u  t  o  s  u  s  o  t
a  i  l  i  t  r  k  m  c  i
l  a  f  u  t  e  t  t  a  t
n  m  m  n  m  e  d  u  y  u
i  e  e  u  f  v  m  l  n  d
d  v  l  p  o  l  l  u  t  e
e  o  e  t  u  l  o  s  b  a
v  u  n  i  f  o  r  m  w  z
```

email
flute
absolute
attitude
pollute
acorn
costume
equal
fortune
uniform

amuse
delete
even
item
volume

Circle the correct spelling of the word

snake snaik snayk

daysy daisy

shaik shayk shake

wayt wait wate

rayn rane rain

gaim game gaym

saim same

afrayd afrade afraid

caym caim came

skate skait skayt

trai tray

hay hai

sprai spray

today todai

sleap sleep slepe

streat street

grean green grene

deleet delete deleat

monkee monkey monkea

hockee hockea hockey

goet goat gote

sope soep soap

boan bone boen

roep roap rope

toyl toil

soil soyl

boy boi

toi toy

my mi

try tri

fluff fluf

kis kiss

buzz buz

bus buss

chef cheff

gass gas

familee familey family

costuum costume costuem

Word bank

snake
tale
sale
shake
mistake
frame
game
same
pane
came
tame
cape
plane
skate

train
daisy
plain
chain
wait
paint
maid
rain
rein
reign
tail
afraid
complain

eat
easy
each
read
Easter
clean
peach
east
neat
deal
tea
least
beast
speak
freak
tweak
yeast
cream
dream
team
jeans
please
cease
crease
grease
leash
weasel
really
feast

sleep
green
keep
street
feet
teeth
wheel
bee
knee (say the sounds k n ee)
tree
sweet
*three
*free
fee
meat
meet
been
bean

We are eating meat tonight when we meet at the restaurant. Different kind of meat....

delete
these
swede
concrete
theme
complete
key
kidney
honey
money
monkey
Disney
Sydney
hockey
jockey

toe
foe
potatoes
tomatoes
heroes
goat
boat
coat
road
oak
soap
loaf
toad

boy
toy
coy
joy
annoy

foe opposite of friend

boil
toil
soil
coin
join
joint
point
hoist
moist
spoil
voice
choice

my
try
fly
fries
pie
tie
die

quest
quit
quick
ill
fluff
kiss
buzz
cuff

tray
hay
clay
stay
spray
day
play
say
crayon
betray
away
today
holiday
hooray

again

Again is spelled the same as the words in this column but sounds different. Focus on "again" here and keep highlighting how different it sounds in a conversation but written the same as these words.

flute
volume
pollute
fortune
attitude
costume
absolute
amuse

These can be harder…come back to them later then.

acorn
uniform
item
equal
ebook
even
delete
program
music
iPad

nose
bone
sole
soul
cone
hope
drone
home
note
globe
tone
envelope
phone
rope

royal
loyal
oyster
voyage
Rolls Royce

glue
true
blue
fruit
suit

study
family
pretty
lucky

kennel
kids

Ask your child to write these words in the form of short spelling tests.

Word bank

 week
weak

7 days in a week (all the days have 24hours). All the same.
He is too weak to pick you up.

 tale
tail

She is telling a tale about the animal`s tail

sale 
sail 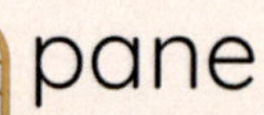

I can buy a new sail for the boat on sale in the shop.
Sail with an "i" reminds us of the knots of the sail.

pa**i**n 
pane 

If the glass pane falls on your foot, you will have pain. Pain is on a specific spot. Window pane.

plane 
plain 

The plane with a plain pattern landed on a plane (flat surface).
The blanket is plain. It has no spots. No pattern.

male 
ma**i**l 

<u>male</u> and fe<u>male</u>

mailbox

mane 
ma**i**n

lion`s mane
main entrance

starter main dessert
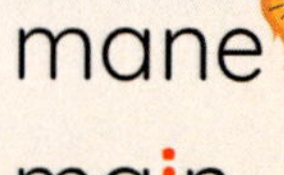
idea  **main** 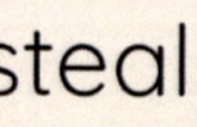 road
 water pipe

 made
ma**i**d

The maid made your bed.

I see the sea in the distance. Big waves and small waves - different.

sea 
see

See with "ee" - you have two eyes that look the same or look at the same time.

flee
flea 

Flee means run away with both feet.
Flea is an insect.

steel 
steal 

If you steal steel you might go to jail.

3 thr**ee**
tr**ee**
fr**ee**

When you are three, you are not free to run where you want.

Ask your child to write these words in the form of short spelling tests.

Spelling test 1

w _ _ _ _ _   (7 days)

p _ _ _ _ _ _   (fly with)

s _ _ _ _ _   (boat with fabric)

m _ _ _ _ _   (man and woman)

p _ _ _ _   (hurt)

s _ _   (beach and waves)

t _ _ _ _ _   (bigger than plants)

st _ _ _   (type of metal)

m _ _ _ _   (hair of lion)

st _ _ _ _ _   (taking things)

k _ _ _   (when we say hello)

f _ _ _ _   (bug on dogs)

m _ _ _ _ box (for post)

s _ _ _   (do with your eyes

Spelling test 2

s _ _ _ _ _   (clean)

ho _ _ _ _ _ _   (vacation)

af _ _ _ _ _ (scared)

poll _ _ _ _   (dirt)

t _ _ _ _ _   (brush them)

m _ _ _   (protein)

m _ _ _ _ _   (animal)

_ _ p _   (media device)

t _ m _ t _ _ s (in salad)

n _ _ _   (face)

d _ _ _ _   (fly in sky)

e _ _ _ _ _ _   (letter)

f _ _ _ _   (chips)

c _ _ _ _ _   (money)

Spelling dictation 1

This week we go on holiday.

We fly with the plane to Sydney.

I can see the sea!

We will spend three days on the beach.

Will you be at Disney?

I can see the tail of the cat.

The dog sleeps in a kennel.

The dog has not one flea on his back.

 If you cannot pick up a glass pane, you are weak.

Spelling dictation 2

I can see a boat with a sail.

The sail has no stripes. It is plain.

The man is free to go. He did not steal the hockey stick.

The male and female bathrooms are over there.

He is happy with the low cost of gas in the sale.

The main pain is in her foot.

She tells a tale of a bee that got stuck in the mailbox.

Spelling dictation 3

The royal king gave the boy a coin for an oyster.

I write a letter with a crayon.

I put it in an envelope.

My family likes to eat swede, honey and meat.

Every meal is a big feast when we are on holiday.

The phone rang at home.

Spelling dictation 4

He wanted to quit his job quietly but quickly they said no.

You have to stand in a queue if you want fries.

His feet were dirty when he ran in the street.

He broke his toenail after the kid with the blue nose chased him.

c   k   or   ck

BEGINNING OF A WORD

General rule......

At the **BEGIN**ning of a word "c" makes a loud "k" sound if followed by

a   o   u

cat   cot   cut

If we want the **BEGIN**ning of the word to be a loud "k" sound but "e" or "i" are the next letter, then the "real" "k"
(also called the kicking "k") comes to the rescue!

e   i

kid   kelp

kiss   Ken

kick   kennel

Kevin

_ at	_ id
_ ot	_ en
_ ut	_ iss
_ash	_ ennel
_ar	_elp

To make the
loud sound "k"

c + a   k + e

c + o   k + i

c + u

cat cot cut

"c" to make the <u>loud</u> sound "k"

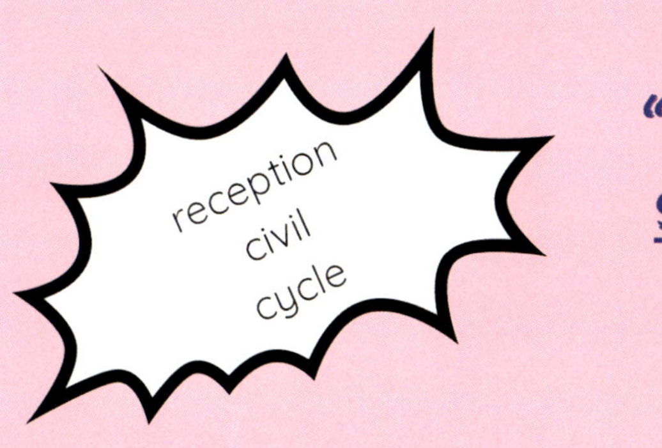

kennel kid kiss
kick kelp

c + a
c + o
c + u

k + e
k + i

reception
civil
cycle

"c" to make the <u>soft</u> sound "s"

c + e
c + i
c + y

We will look in detail at the soft sound of "c" in the next book.

c   k   or   ck

At the **END** of a <u>SHORT VOWEL SOUND</u> word (and mimics of it) we add **ck** for the **loud** "k" sound

pack
socks
lock
sack
backpack
rack
lack

- "a" is a short vowel sound in pack...so we add "c" & "k" = "ck"

stock
rock 
suck
luck
*lucky
clock
truck
**wreck 
click

- * In the word "lucky" you can hear the {E} sound at the end of the word. We most often just write "y" for this sound at the end of a word

- ** w+r is challenging ...we will approach it later.

If the vowel says its name

{A} {E} {I} {O} {U} in the word, use the kicking "k" to mae the loud "k" sound.

The letter "e" at the end of the word, makes the vowel say its name.

fake bake brake cake
broke stroke

Come back to these when more is known about the vowel saying its name.

Use "k" **AFTER** a consonant

pink drink blink sink shark park
dark trunk blank prank sank

This rule will become very apparent as we move along.

If it is too challenging, come back to this later.

Are these really exceptions? The loud "c" sound is after a consonant. So we write the "c" sound with a kicking "k".

eg. skull
skunk

When "c" is followed by "e" , "i" or "y",
it makes a soft sound "s".

c + e   **reception**
c + i   **civil**
c + y   **cycle**

We just mention the "s" sound for "c" here as we will recall this rule in the next book. (Reading purposes only at this point.)

bicycle
recycle
cyclone
civil
cell
reception
received
princess
cell
cellphone

circus
cellar
certain
cellular
city
centre
cylinder
celery
Cyprus
circle

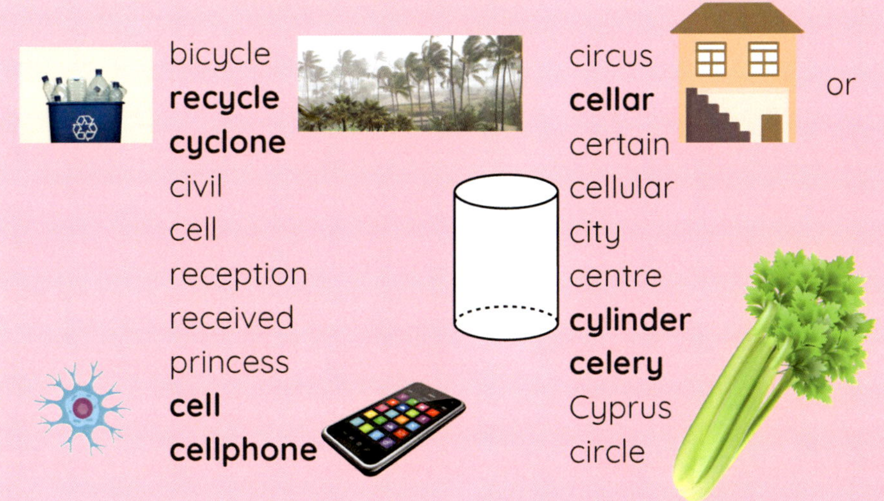

or

These are more challenging words, but they should be talked about.

The same story for the letter "g", but we will look at that later.

Repeat! Repeat! Repeat!

c   k   ck   or   the soft sound c summary

1. At the beginning of a word

- cat
- cot
- cut

 But if the "c" sound is followed by an "e" or "i" then we need to use the kicking "k" to make a loud "c" sound!

- kiss
- kennel

2. At the end of a word with a single <u>short vowel sound</u> **(and mimics of it) we add "ck" to make the loud "c" sound:**

- pack
- socks
- clock
- truck
- wreck
- click

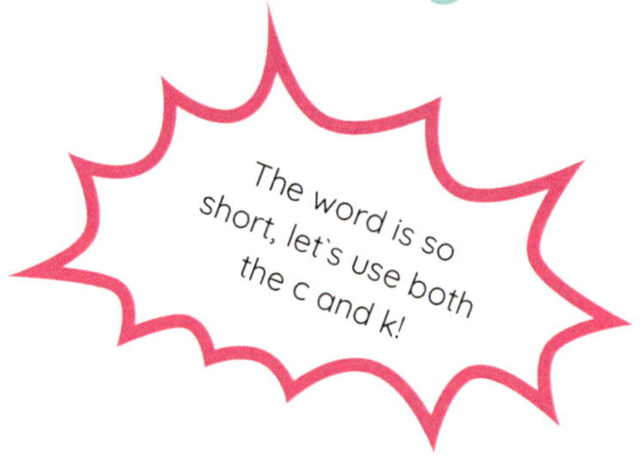

3. If the vowel says its name {A} {E} {O} {I} {U} in the word, then use the "k" to make the "loud" "k" sound.

fake bake brake cake
broke stroke

4. Use "k" AFTER a consonant

pink drink blink sink shark park dark
skunk trunk blank prank sank

 5. Are these really exceptions? The loud "c" sound is after a consonant. So we write the "c" sound with a kicking "k".

eg. skull
skunk

When "c" is followed by an "e", "i" or "y" it makes a different sound "soft" "s".

c + e   reception
c + i   ➡   civil
c + y   cycle

Draw a line from the picture to the correct letter(s) to make the "k" sound.

There is a note to the left to help with this exercise. The next page is the same exercise without the note.

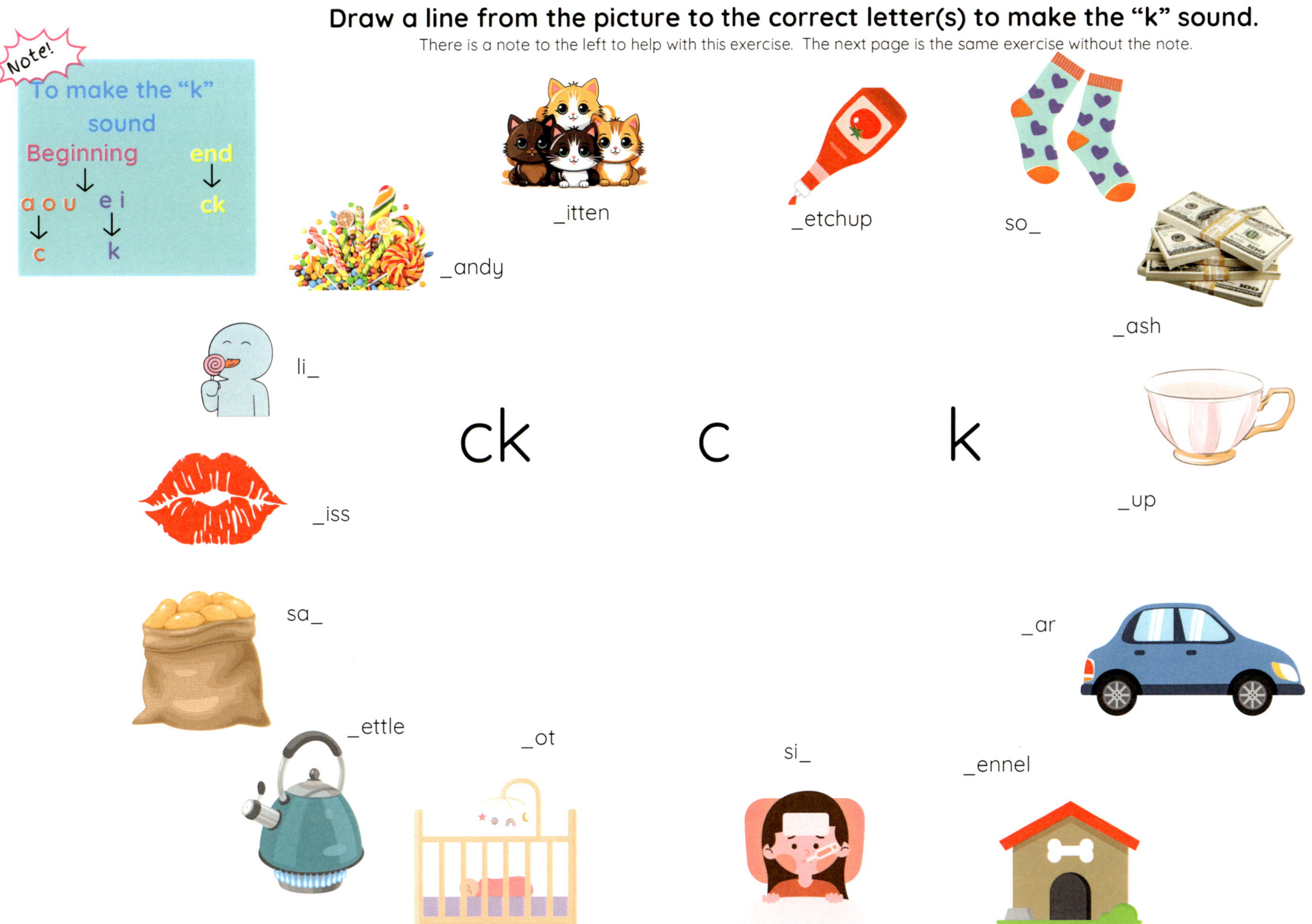

Crossword
Add c k or ck

Across

1. ba_

3. _ut

4. _ane

6. _at

7. _ids

9. _ennel

10. _ot

Down

2. _ute

3. _andy

4. che_

5. _utter

6. _an

8. sa_

9. _ettle

Answers at the back of the book.

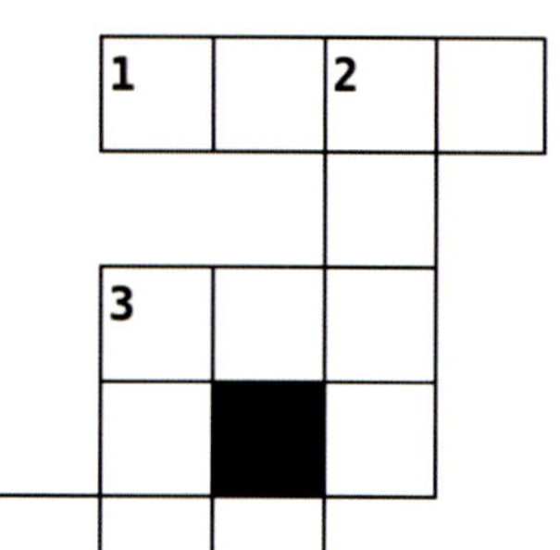

Draw a line from the picture to the correct letter(s) to make the "k" sound.

ck   c   k

ketchup socks cash cup car kennel sick cat kettle sock kiss lick candy kittens

Circle the correct spelling of the word

rak rack rac

bake bace backe

nek neck nec

skunk scunc scunk

sckeleton sceleton skeleton

kit cit ckit

kut cut ckut

cill ckill kill

bacpak backpack

suc suck suk

kandy ckandy candy

cetchup cketchup ketchup

kettle cettle ckettle

Word bank

rack
back
sack
backpack
lack
lick
flick
click
slick
trick
neck
suck
tuck
luck
sock
mock

vs

can
cost
candy
cutter
canteen

leek
creek
soak
bake
rake
make

kill
skill
kiss
***kit**
***kid**
kennel

skeleton
sky
ski

skull
skunk

acid
cent
cell
centre
pencil
city
cycle
central
celebrate
citrus
civil

Be aware of the sound the **"c"** makes when followed by an **i e y** →

We learn to spell these in the next book

bicycle

prince
prince**ss***

cyber

Prince and princess are more challenging to write.

qu.......queen

The "q" [kwh] is ALWAYS written together
with a "u"

q + u

Write quit quite quiet at the same time. Decide which one is which.
- quit   "i" is a short vowel sound
- quite The "e" at the end makes "i" says its name {I}
- quiet Emphasise the sound of "e".

quaint	*quit
quest	*quite
quench	*quiet
quantity	quota
squishy	quote
squirrel	quilt
request	quack
equips	quay
equal	squash

*

- There are a lot of spelling rules applied in these words. Try and find them all.
- "ai" says its name {A} in quaint
- When you hear the {E} sound at end of a word, you often write it with a "y". like in "quantity".
- Equips & equal: open vowel syllable so the vowel says its name {E}.

Study the words and see which ones are challenging to write and how will you remember it (place an anchor).

squirt
squirrel
inquisitive
acquaintance
quarrel
require
queen

mosquito

mosquito**es**

You will never forget this one again!

queue .... break it up ....q + ue + ue

qu.......queen

qu + i + t = quit

qu + i + t + e = quite (i saying {I})

qu + i + e + t = quiet
(put accent on "e" when you say it)

Just for revision: cute and q +ue +ue

What is the difference between quack and quake?
Can you write them both?

An " e" on the end of quake makes the vowel say its name {A} (like "A" in acorn). Whereas, the "a" in quack is the short vowel sound "a" (like "a" for apple) so it finishes with a "ck" at the end of the word.

Word search

```
e u l k w e q y k r q k e e n
c h c n e u q u t o s e q t l
n u z v q u t s i i q h u i e
a d x z z r q t i v t i a u r
t b t l i u e d c p e n l q r
n o d u i i n l d c r r a p i
i l q s u t q u o t e a w u u
a s h q r u i s q u a s h g q
u y u r d e y u u u z b g p s
q d r a y t q s q n e m r d l
c e b q i b t u c b p u b g q
a g a l k b h q e d u q e l d
t t a p e v i t i s i u q n i
u u e j m o s q u i t o e s x
q n v m i b o z o d x v v z l
```

acquaintance
mosquitoes
quench
quit
quote
squirrel
equal
quality
quite
squirt
quiver
squash
squishy
request

Spelling test

Floss (zz) rule

If a one syllable word has only one vowel and ends in f, l, or s, z then we **double** the **last** letter.

moss boss sniff kiss stuff cuff bill fill chill drill glass grass cliff toss buzz fizz

This includes a two syllable word ACTING like a one syllable word.
flossing crosses kisses glasses bosses bossing grassing buzzing

….grassing on them to the local police

A few exceptions to the rule we do learn here, as they arrive early
in our vocabulary list: **gas yes this us bus plus chef**

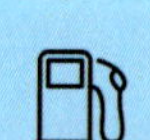

ll
all
fall
tall
small

Only one
always
already
almost
although
altogether

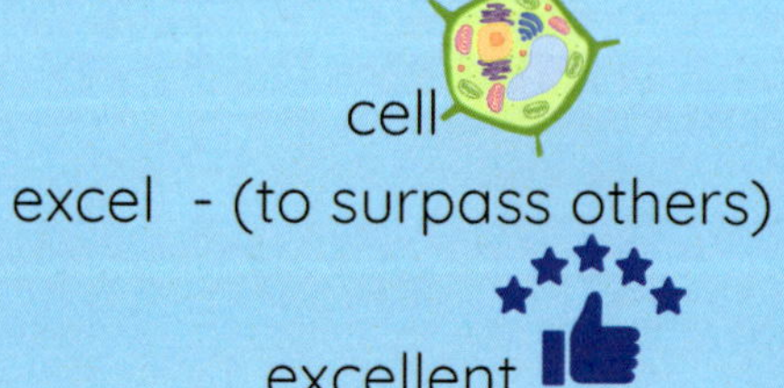

cell
excel - (to surpass others)

excellent

excel
excel +ing = excelling
(excelled)

The word "excel" is very unique without a double "l"

Only add a double consonant if needed

flos

bus

fluf

mis

kids

buz

yes

bil

gras

gas

glas

us

plus

kis

chef

this

dril

chil

stuf

tos

snif

floss bus fluff miss kids buzz yes bill grass gas glasss us plus kiss chef this drill chill stuff toss sniff

Homophones 

Learn these four words together. Write "peas" three different ways and tell me which one is which. Then write please.

Can I have a piece of cake?
The strawberry is the "i" on the cake.

piece

peas

The "e" makes peace with the "a".

peace

please

Homophones

Write these words again without looking at the previous page.

A slice of cake is called a _ ?

- -

This vegetable is good for you.

- -

Not war, but _ ?

- -

Remember your manners, say _ and _ .

- -

Crossword answers

Crossword answers

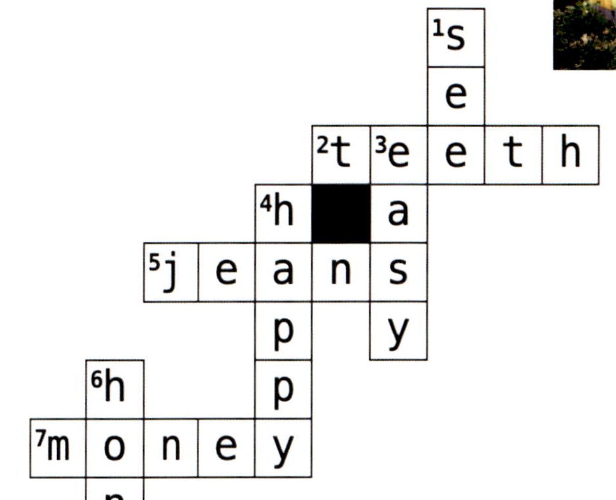

															1 s		
															e		
													2 t	3 e	e	t	h
												4 h	■	a			
										5 j	e	a	n	s			
												p		y			
									6 h			p					
								7 m	o	n	e	y					
					8 p				n								
					e				e								
				9 f	a	m	i	l	y								
					c												
				10 s	h	e	e	p									
				w													
11 h	o	c	k	e	y												
				d													
	12 t	h	r	e	e												

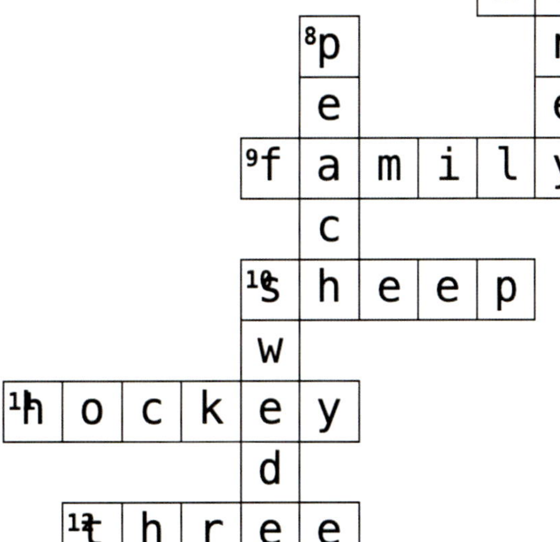

Crossword answers

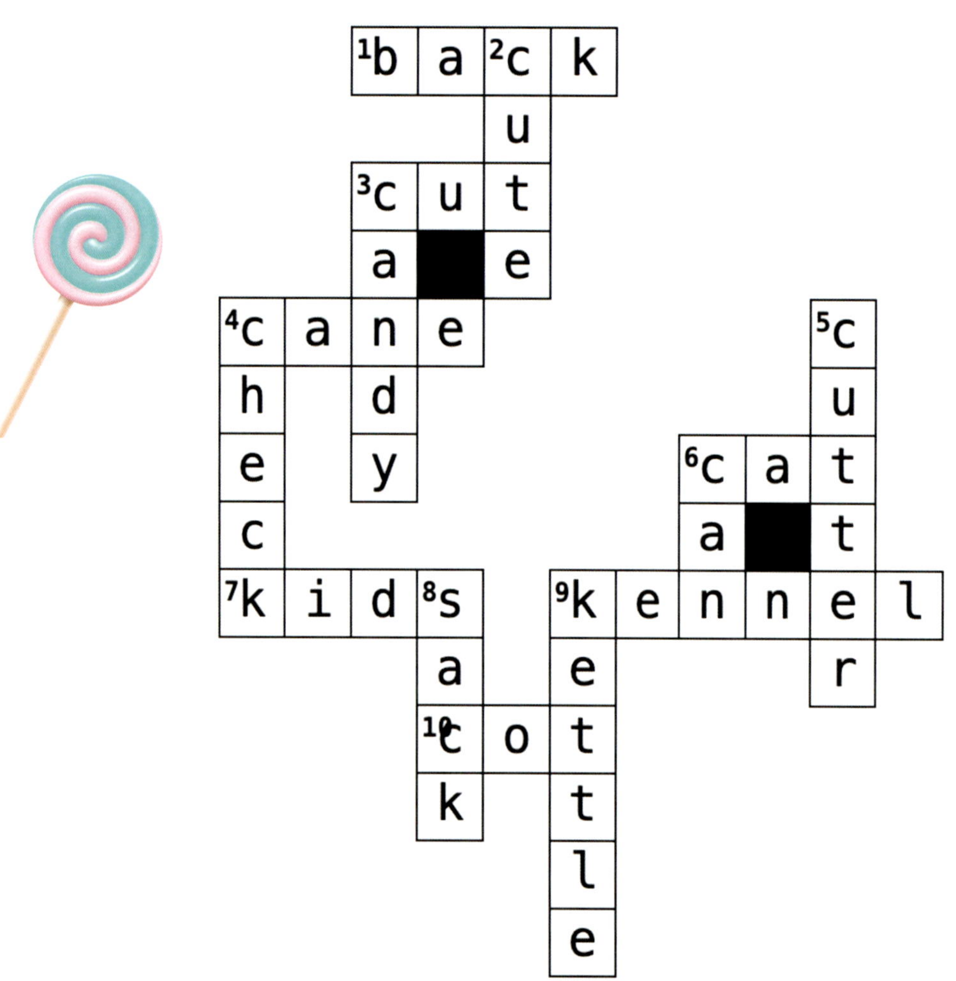

Reward chart (stamp or colour in)

A Logical Approach to Spelling

You can contact us by email at
info@logicalapproachtolearning.com
You can follow us on Instagram
logicalapproachtospelling
2024 Jurina Dean